BRATZ™

First published by Parragon in 2007
Parragon
Queen Street House
4 Queen Street
Bath BA1 1HE, UK

ISBN 978-1-4054-8743-6

Printed in China

TRADING FACES

CLICK!

CLICK!

CLICK!

Just back from Brazil, Fianna shows off her awesome samba moves. Cameron can barely keep up with his camera.

Sasha shows the other Bratz her stylin' samba moves.

You're lookin' at the next winner of the Club Mambo dance contest!

Cool, Sasha! You're entering too?

Dylan shows the Bratz some of his slick dance moves...

Cloe gives Dylan a piece of her mind.

Are you crazy, Dylan? You almost hit Fianna!

Dylan feels like a total fool.

Dylan complains to Cameron about his luck with the ladies.

The Bratz get in some blading time. Sasha asks the others if they'll help her for the dance contest. Jade and Cloe will help, but they've agreed to help Fianna too!

Sasha is more than a little annoyed.

Cameron finds himself an unwanted admirer. He makes a quick getaway...

But this admirer is not all she seems.

Nice to meet you. Later!

Dude, chill. It's me. Your best bud, Dylan!

Cloe asks Cameron about his new friend.

Oh. Um... that's Delilah. Dylan's very shy country cousin.

Always friendly, Fianna introduces herself. Dylan/Delilah puts on his/ her best female voice.

The Bratz ask where Dylan is.

Fianna tells Delilah she should definitely join the contest.

To Cameron's surprise, "Delilah" agrees.

Yeah, no problem!

I'll do it... if you'll show me some moves.

Several hours later...

Cameron has to admit—Dylan looks like a girl!

I bet you say that to all the boys.

But Delilah is still not very graceful!

Kirstee and Kaycee arrive at the wrong time.

Like, who's the klutz?

Celebrity judge for the dance contest, Byron Powell, suddenly appears. He thinks Delilah is beautiful.

And your name is...

"Delilah" introduces "herself". Cameron tells Byron Delilah is entering the dance contest.

Byron is thrilled. He tells Delilah that his music company is always looking for dancers.

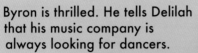

We must do lunch!

Delilah tells Byron "she" is with Cameron, but Cameron totally bails.

Thanks, but no thanks.

Splendid! Shall we?

Delilah is starting to freak!

Kaycee and Kirstee cannot believe Byron has fallen for Delilah!

We're gonna enter that dance contest and win!

Meanwhile, at lunch, Byron tells Delilah "she" has star quality.

Delilah doesn't know what to say. Luckily Fianna walks past...

She waves to Delilah.

Delilah accidentally drops her napkin on the floor.

Excuse me! I'll be right back.

As Byron scans the menu for mega triple burgers, Delilah sneaks off to find Fianna.

Fianna can't believe Delilah is having lunch with Byron Powell.

While Kirstee works out how to stop the machine, Sasha works out her dance moves.

But Sasha won't play ball.

Sasha gives the Bratz a piece of her mind!

My BFFs are stylin' my competitor —and I'M overreacting?

YES!

Sasha takes off.

Later!

This is taking way too long.

Finally off the bicep machine, the Tweevils continue their workout.

Kirstee hits a button, sending the machines into overdrive.

AAAAGH!

Lunch finished, Fianna leaves the restaurant.

Delilah, waiting outside, disturbs Fianna with a burp.

Must have been the triple burger!

Fianna is sorry for hurting Dylan's feelings.

Be back in a sec!

Wait! I'll get him!!

Delilah runs back into the restaurant to get "Dylan."

Fianna and Sasha watch as Delilah takes off.

Later!

Still angry at the others for helping Fianna, Sasha follows close behind.

A couple of seconds after, Dylan bursts through the beads.

Hey, ladies!

Dylan immediately breaks it down for the Bratz, spinning and twisting his body.

The Dylman is back!

Jade can't understand where Delilah has gotten to.

She headed over to the club.

Dylan, weary from all the running and trading faces, flops on the chair.

The Bratz decide they have to go to the contest without Delilah.

Fianna drags Dylan off the chair.

Burdine lectures the Tweevils on what to do when they win the dance contest.

The Tweevils, exhausted after all their exercise, can't even move.

Burdine is fuming.

Sasha totally blows the audience away with her stylin' moves!

Byron Powell immediately announces the next contestant—it's Delilah!

Delilah leaps and spins across the stage.

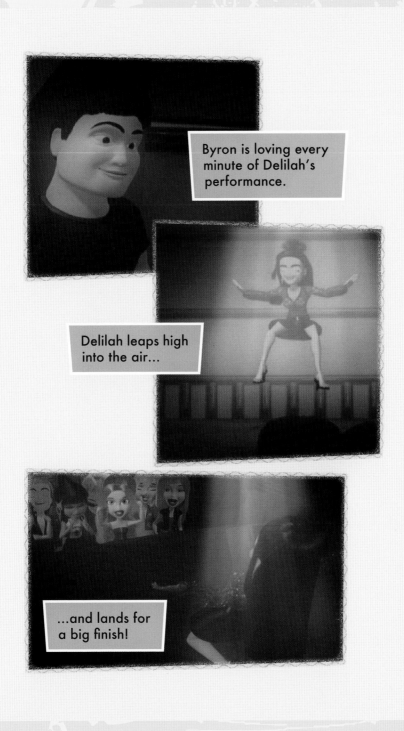

Byron is loving every minute of Delilah's performance.

Delilah leaps high into the air...

...and lands for a big finish!

Fianna starts showing off her stylin' samba moves!

She is totally kickin' it!

And the audience knows it!

The Tweevils weren't lying—they totally CANNOT dance!

Exhausted, they collapse on stage.

The unthinkable happens—two of Delilah's "props" bounce onto the stage!

The Bratz aren't quite sure what is going on—but it ain't cool!

Delilah does "her" best to regain her composure.

Delilah is back into the swing of things in no time...

... and wowing the crowd with "her" moves.

And then Delilah's "props" bounce onto the stage again!

Byron is in total shock—this can't be happening!

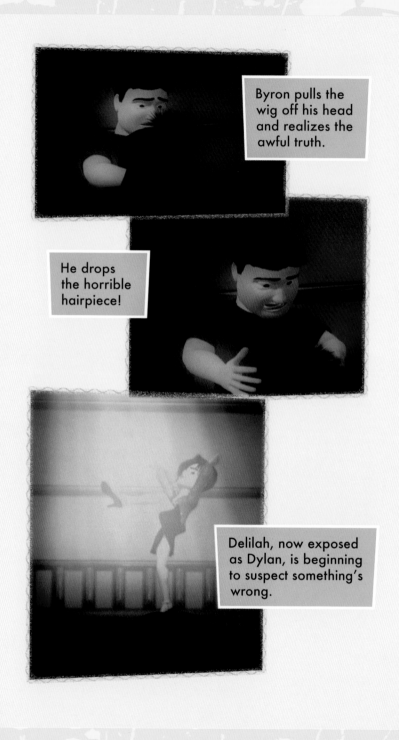

Dylan suddenly realizes his plan—along with his costume—has fallen apart!

The shock worn off, the audience bursts into fits of hysterics!

But things only get worse for Dylan...

The Bratz enter the magazine office to find a surprise waiting for them.

It's Sasha—she's decorated the studio to celebrate Fianna's win!

What? You're splittin'?

Dylan's joy soon turns to horror!

Dylan reminds Fianna of all he had to go through—tight clothes, dancing in high heels...

Sasha, smiling, turns on some music—it's time to party!

So the Dylman went through torture for just one date.

And the girls made me write an article about it in *Bratz* magazine!

BRATZ™

YASMIN™

Sometimes Yasmin can be a little quiet, but even without her saying a word, you can sense this girl's special. There's just something about her that seems almost regal. But Yasmin's not pretentious! She's really open-minded—she's always up on alternative trends in fashion, fitness, and beauty!
Nickname: Pretty Princess

SASHA™

Sasha's not afraid of confrontation—she knows who she is, what she wants, and how to get it! Fashion's a huge part of her life, but music is even more important to "Bunny Boo!" Someday you can be sure she'll be a record producer... with her own fashion line!
Nickname: Bunny Boo

JADE™

Always on the cutting edge of cool, Jade's the ultimate fashionista! After checking out the latest fashion mags, the trendiest boutiques, and all the thrift stores, she always manages to put together looks that are completely unique and just scream "Kool Kat!"
Nickname: Kool Kat

CLOE™

Cloe's so creative that her whole life has become a work of art, from designing fantastic fashions to creating cool new cosmetic looks to her tendency to be dramatic! Sometimes her imagination runs away with her, but her friends help this "Angel" stay grounded!
Nickname: Angel

FIANNA™

Fianna may be a funky fashionista, but she's also way down to earth. She has some super-sweet dance moves, and she always makes the dance floor her own. Fianna's called "Fragrance" because she's as sweet as she smells.
Nickname: Fragrance

BRATZ™